SUCCESS

Other books by Michele Thornton Ghee

Stratechic: Life & Career-Winning Strategies for Women

Stratechic 2.0: Her Plan. Her Power. Her Purpose.

SUCCESS
ON YOUR TERMS

MICHELE THORNTON GHEE

MYND
MATTERS

Books may be purchased in quantity and/or special sales by
contacting the author at
www.michelethorntonghee.com

Published by
Mynd Matters Publishing
715 Peachtree Street NE
Suites 100 & 200
Atlanta, GA 30308
www.myndmatterspublishing.com

ISBN-13: 978-1-948145-29-9 (pbk)
978-1-948145-31-2 (eBook)

FIRST EDITION

Printed in the United States of America

Cover photo by Maya Darasaw, M.A.D. Works Photography
Hair by Will Rob Hair
Makeup by Bre Khounphinith

Tony, Taylor, and Jordan
You are my inspiration
to change the world,
one success story at a time.

To my father, the late Walt Thornton,
I'm living out the promise.

To my mother, Francoise, and my brother,
David, thank you for your love
and support.

Proud Product of Oakland, California.

SUCCESS

/səkˈses/

noun

The accomplishment of an aim or purpose.

To achieve a goal.

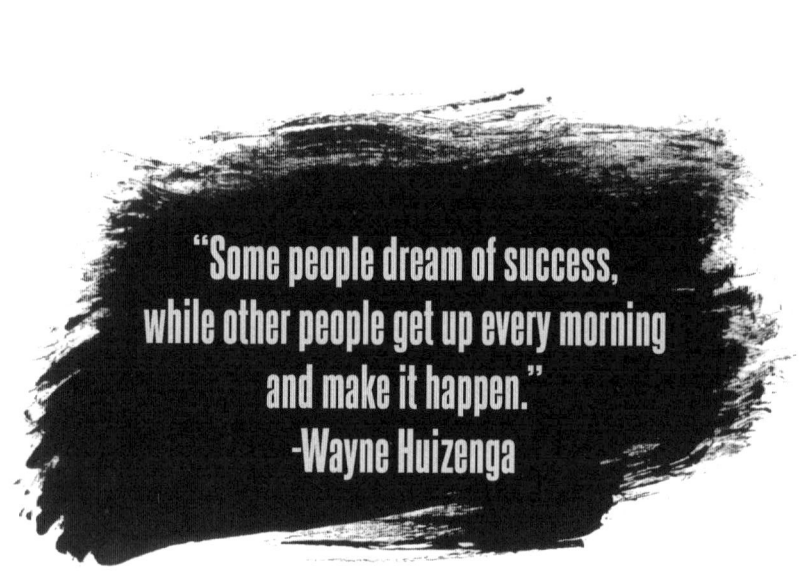

"Some people dream of success,
while other people get up every morning
and make it happen."
-Wayne Huizenga

INTRODUCTION

When I searched for "success" online, I got roughly 2,970,000,000 results. Likely because everyone has a different definition of what it looks like and how to achieve it. You as an individual, your company, the people in your life, others in the world—all have a different perception of what it means to be successful. Usually, the definition stops short of being about its actual attainment and instead rests on the *appearance* of having it or becoming it. Appearance is subjective and really not the best way to determine true success.

It's a shame we rarely get a chance to define success for our own lives. Instead, we try to live up to other people's standards by accepting their terms and conditions. Without much struggle, we submit to another's vision for our lives and then wonder how everything gets screwed up and off track. We feel drained and defeated and have no idea how to get back to where we know we should be. Most people aren't unhappy or "unsuccessful" because they're lazy. I believe they don't achieve success or at least envision themselves as successful because they ceded their power to everyone else and saw little value in defining such a simple yet powerful concept for themselves.

Instead of relying on what others think of you or envision for you, I want you to define SUCCESS ON YOUR TERMS one achievement at a time.

THE REAL QUESTIONS ARE: What is your goal? How will you achieve it?

What is YOUR definition of success for YOURself?

Think for a moment. What dreams did you have when you were a child? What about as a young adult? Now, think about your life—all of it. What are the beautiful elements that make it unique and inspiring?

If you took out a sheet of paper and drew a "success ladder" with failure and disappointment at the bottom and success at the top, where would you place yourself? Would your decision be based on your personal definitions or what others think?

Have you spent more time bending to the wants and will of others or are you living life on _your_ terms? Really consider your perception of **SUCCESS**. How does it show up? How would you describe it today? Next year? Ten years from now?

Do you know how to accomplish the goals you set for yourself? What about the people needed to help you get there? Do you have the courage to see it through even when things are complicated and tiring? What about your timeline?

SUCCESS: ON YOUR TERMS is a guide to amplify your voice and path and silence opinions and ideas that no longer serve you or truly align with what you want for your life.

I've heard people say the media and entertainment industry is filled with a bunch of C students living an A+ lifestyle. I can't say if they are right or wrong but I can say my own road to success has been quite a journey. One filled with a bunch of ideas and thoughts that somehow all landed on a piece of paper that became this book. When I looked down and noticed the most important building blocks started with the letter C, I realized I was on to something. As you flip through these pages, you will notice that each section is based on a concept and each concept begins with the letter C.

SUCCESS: ON YOUR TERMS requires openness and honesty. Not with me, with yourself. It's about accountability and giving yourself the freedom to define what you want in your life and from your life. Because if you don't choose a destination, you will always find yourself wandering around aimlessly without foundation or focus, seeking something you may not even want in the end. It's a journey, not a destination. It's time to put *you* at the Center of your success!

Two years ago, my executive assistant, Brittney Dorsette, gifted me a copy of *The Circle Maker* by Mark Batterson and asked me to read it. At the time, I thanked her for her generosity but quickly pushed the book to the bottom of my to-do list because I was too busy for casual reading. A couple of months later, right before I left home for a flight from New York to California, I saw the book sitting on my kitchen counter and decided to take it just in case I grew tired of watching movies on the plane.

The first chapter hit me fast and hard, I could barely brace my mind and emotions for its impact. I read each word until I reached the last page and felt my perspective shifting. It is the type of book that changes lives over the course of several pages (as I hope this book does for you). *The Circle Maker* inspired me to write down my goals and draw a circle around them. The book motivated me to make my prayers and expectations bigger and bolder.

Every morning I got down on my knees and prayed audacious prayers with specifics of what I wanted to have manifest in my life. My list of circled goals was at the Center of every prayer.

Written boldly across the top were three letters, E-V-P. I had earned and asked for the title of Executive Vice President because I'd gone above and beyond and perfected the idea of doing more and getting results. I'd also exceeded my revenue goals. God promised me growth and I was not afraid to leave my then-role in anticipation of what God was going to deliver. I had been with my previous employer for six years and had done some amazing work like being the architect of the first and only network for black women. As a matter of fact, I was so confident about my decision to walk in the direction of EVP because part of my prayer was that I asked God to close any door not covered by His will and grace. It sounds easy but it is a tough prayer to have God actually close doors firmly before or behind you. He's closed some doors I was positive had my first and last name engraved in the wood!

Today, I am the Executive Vice President of Business Development at Endeavor Global Marketing and I know my assistant's gift, along with everything I am about to share, was integral in reaching my goal. My assistant changed my life with a simple gesture and I pray this book has a similar impact for you. It is filled with thoughts, guidance, inspiration, understanding, realness, and a call to action. It includes the checklist I've used for my last three major life moves and clearly defined strategies to enable you to get what you've earned. One thing I learned many years ago is that there is no one to blame if my dreams don't pan out except myself. It is on each of us to build our own escape route, to walk in our destiny, or to change the course of our lives one **SUCCESS** at a time.

We are responsible for our actions, reactions, choices, and decisions.

SUCCESS is a powerful word and the CC's are its building blocks. This book, much like the word itself, is built on those CC's. They are evident in the contract that I demand you sign before jumping into the core concepts as well as the courage it will take to see your commitment through to success. They are the clarity you will discover and the unexpected champion to help you along your journey. I ask you to be a coach but more importantly, to be coachable. However, in the end, it's your choice whether your life will be a success based on your terms.

CLEAR YOUR MIND.

CHOOSE TO BE SUCCESSFUL.

COMMIT TO THE PROCESS.

CELEBRATE THE VICTORY.

L E T ' S G O ! ! !

WHAT ARE YOU TRYING TO ACHIEVE?

A Promotion

More Money

Recognition

A Bigger Title

Starting A New Business

Making Your Company Look Good

Losing Weight

Getting Married

Being Financially Free

Being A Great Stay-At-Home Mom

Being A Great Working Mom

Being A Great Dad

Getting Good Grades

Volunteering in Your Community

Having 100k Social Media Followers

There is **POWER** and **CLARITY** when you write out the goal you want to achieve. It is proven that writing out your goals inspires you to take action. You have to be specific.

Example: I want to be promoted in 60 days to VP of Operations.

Example: I want to create a personal board of directors in 90 days.

Example: I want to lose 20 pounds in 2 months by giving up sugar and bread. I will only eat on a small plate for each meal.

Example: I will carve out 1 hour a week to journal. I will use what I write to improve my relationships.

Goal I Want to Achieve_____

Action(s) I Will Take_____

Goal Will Be Achieved By_____

This book is <u>not</u> about business.
It is about the business of defining and
executing your vision of SUCCESS
one achievement at a time.

MY DEFINITION OF **SUCCESS** FOR MY LIFE MATTERS MOST AND NOT THAT OF OTHERS. OTHERS GET NO ENERGY BECAUSE THAT IS ENERGY TO BE USED FOR <u>MY</u> PATH AND <u>MY</u> DESTINY.

As you read, keep in mind two very essential points.

POINT 1: **THIS IS NOT THE BOOK OF WANTS.**

POINT 2: **THIS IS THE BOOK OF ACTION!**

SUCCESS GUIDE

COMMITMENT

The state or quality of being dedicated to a cause, activity, etc.

The state of being loyal to **YOURSELF**.

"DESIRE IS THE
KEY TO MOTIVATION, BUT
IT'S DETERMINATION AND COMMITMENT TO AN
UNRELENTING PURSUIT OF YOUR GOAL, A COMMITMENT TO
EXCELLENCE, THAT WILL ENABLE YOU TO ATTAIN
THE SUCCESS YOU SEEK."
-MARIO ANDRETTI

This is **BIGGER** than a commitment to the process. It's a commitment to **YOURSELF**.

Commitment to wake up every day with purpose

Commitment to put yourself first

Commitment to carve out 1 hour a day for yourself

to achieve the goals you listed

Commitment to remove people who only take

and don't give back

Commitment to a no-guilt policy for your life

Commitment to be honest with yourself daily

Commitment to keep going when faced

with conflict

"Success is not final; Failure is not fatal.
It is the courage to continue that counts."
-Winston Churchill

COURAGE

Taking an honest assessment of your life takes courage.

Do you like what you see?

Always remember, even if you are super successful and think you have everything, as long as you have breath in your body, the game is not over.

Why is courage important?

Courage is the antidote to fear. Both cannot live within you at the same time.

How do you get courage?

You make a daily decision that courage will reside where fear once lived. Practice a courageous act every day for 30 days. Write out what it is and the results it produced.

To not be perfect takes **COURAGE**

COURAGE to walk in your value

The **COURAGE** to move forward after you've failed

The **COURAGE** to admit you don't know everything

The **COURAGE** to leave the past behind you

The **COURAGE** to forgive

The **COURAGE** to give people the benefit of the doubt

The **COURAGE** to activate willpower

The **COURAGE** to ask for help

The **COURAGE** to leave when you don't feel valued

To leave a job I really loved took courage. I had to look at myself in the mirror and honestly answer, "Am I valued? Do I have a seat at the table I helped build?" And the painful answer was no. I knew I couldn't stay. I wasn't respected. That meant that I wouldn't produce at the top of my ability because they took away my purpose. I also knew that it's easier to get a job while you have a job. The first thing I did was activate courage. Then I called one of my biggest champions! The rest is history.

To commit to something and see it through takes **Courage.**

To ask for what you've earned takes **Courage.**

To leave a bad situation takes **Courage.**

To be open and vulnerable takes **Courage.**

To take an honest look at your life takes **Courage.**

To be willing to fail takes **Courage.**

To get back up takes **MORE Courage.**

To eat and live healthy takes **Courage.**

To say **NO** takes **Courage.**

To say **YES** takes **Courage.**

To sign this contract takes **Courage.**

Are you Ready?

CONTRACT

The contract comes after you've made a commitment to yourself and found the courage to no longer accept what is and push ahead towards what can be. It is a symbol to God of your faithfulness and desire for Him to cause shifts in the supernatural so your current patterns can be disrupted and you can continue with a new mindset and a renewed strength.

This contract is personal and only requires one signature, yours. No lawyers will call if you break it and you will be the main person impacted if you decide not to follow through.

Are you willing to be bold enough to make a contract with yourself to become successful? Sign the back of this page if you want more, choose more, and are willing to do the work to have more. It is a commitment to add *action* to your dreams and prayers.

I will determine what success means to me based on *my* wants, needs, goals, desires and not that of others.

_____

(Signature)

_____

(Date)

YTIRAJC

*Clearness or lucidity as to
perception or understanding ;
freedom from indistinctness or ambiguity.*

AND THEN IT ALL FELL IN PLACE.

~CLARITY.

YOU DON'T HAVE TO KNOW
EVERYTHING BUT AT LEAST KNOW
THAT YOU WANT MORE!

"THERE ARE FEW THINGS MORE POWERFUL THAN A LIFE LIVED WITH PASSIONATE CLARITY."
-ERWIN MCMANUS

In November 2017, it was clear to me that I needed to make some decisions about my career. I was at a standstill. I sat at my desk to write out the strategy for my next promotion. I knew the equation for upward movement because I'd used the same strategy for previous jobs with great success. No matter what you are trying to achieve, this formula will help you get from where you are to where you want to go.

- Be **COMMITTED** to the process but more importantly, be **COMMITTED** to your growth

- **COMMIT** to writing out your strategy and working on it every day

- Make sure you use **CLARITY** to look at all of the facts and details about your situation and options

- The fastest way to get what you want is to find a champion to pave the way (remember, make it easy for the **CHAMPION** to work on your behalf by writing all correspondence for them)

- **COURAGE** is critical when it's time to make a decision about asking for what you've earned or leaving a job that's not the right fit

- **CHOOSE** to follow-up in writing so you can hold people accountable

I knew the TV business was shrinking because people had many more options for viewing content. Although I had earned a promotion, because of the business environment it wasn't possible. I decided to ask for a promotion even though I knew a position was not available and they would not create a new role for me. I knew the details and asked anyway. The goal was to let my company know I expected more.

Asking questions helps you gain clarity about how your company or a person feels about you. It allows you to make an educated decision.

The answer was simple. Although there was no room for me to grow, I was told that I was valuable to the company. For me, that wasn't enough. You have decide when you've had enough. All I know is actions speak louder than words. In that moment, I had to make a tough decision. Was it time to leave a job I had built from the ground up—a brand that I truly respected? Should I take a risk and go someplace where I had to start over? Did I have the courage to make a move?

Before any decision, any ask, or any move, there must be **CLARITY**.

Not long ago, I attended one of my favorite women's conferences. That year the conference was held in Southern California (the prior year it was in Florida). After I checked into my room, I headed down to the cocktail reception and the first person I saw was Hilda. She works for the Marriott chain of hotels and was a member of the wait staff in Florida. I couldn't believe it because Hilda lives in Florida. She told me the conference producers called the President of Marriott and requested that Hilda be able to work at the conference no matter the city as long as it's a Marriott property. They explained that the conference would not be a success without her there. The women have come to rely on Hilda and she is part of the conference. I have never met anyone who understands customer service like Hilda. Her title and uniform does not dictate her success. She is one of the most successful people I know.

Your success doesn't have to look like someone else's.

CLARITY

is not a destination but an exercise
on your journey of being honest
with yourself.

Get quiet and ask and ANSWER these questions:

What makes me happy?

What are my strengths and weaknesses?

What adjectives best describe me?
(e.g., leader, assertive, reliable, connector, creative, driven, focused) If you don't create your own adjectives, they will be assigned to you by others. **80% of the decisions made about you happen when you aren't in the room!**

Am I operating at the highest level of my ability?

Is there competition inside and outside and if so, who is it? What is it?

Have I earned more than I've received?

Have I spent enough time in my current role? Do I know what's necessary to move forward?

Do I know the people who are the decision-makers for what I want? Can and will they help me?

What is my timing to ask for what I've earned?

Who is guiding me with my strategy and decisions?

Am I walking in fear or facts?

Culture Eats Strategy.

CULTURE

The behaviors and beliefs characteristic of a particular social, ethnic, or age group.

Back in 2016, I published Stratechic: Life & Career Winning Strategies for Women. Between research obtained for the book and my own professional experiences, I've learned a strategy only works if you understand the culture.

For example, let's say you work in the tech industry and you wear a suit to work every day but everyone else wears jeans. What does your culture say about dress code, demeanor, classroom ethics, or play group rules for the kids? What about meeting formats, communicating with executives, required work hours, children in the office, etc.?

Every job has unwritten cultural nuances and ways of operating. Do you know yours? If you don't, you will NEVER get ahead. The strategy you build for yourself is based on the CULTURAL landscape of your environment. Success lies at the intersection of culture and the strategy you create to win.

What's your current culture?

Who influences the culture?

Are you aligned with your culture?

What do you need to change to succeed in your culture?

Are you willing to change? If not, why?

Can you still be authentic in your current culture? If the answer is no, you have to decide if this is the right environment for you and be prepared to make a smart, courageous, calculated move.

CHANGE

To make or become different.

Change takes courage.

Change is inevitable.

Change is painful.

Change is critical for growth.

Change is necessary.

Change before they ask you to change.

Without Change, growth is impossible.

Change authentically.

I stopped asking to Change them and asked God to Change me!

Control the Change narrative.

There are two parts to Change - you and them.

YOU

What do you need to change about yourself? How can you change your environment with your tools? Who can give you honest feedback about areas of growth? How much time will it take for you to change?

I had to change physically and mentally before I could walk in my success.

I had to change how I used food to hide the pain of not fitting in.

I had to change how I reacted to people's foolishness.

I had to change how and when I showed up at work, meetings, and events.

I had to change and become more honest with myself.

I had to change who I asked for feedback and find truth tellers.

I asked myself what do I need to change in order to win.

In 1997, I changed my life. I promised my dad on his deathbed that I would make him proud of me. To do so meant I had to change how I viewed myself, how I lived, and who I hung out with, to name a few. Back then, I dated the wrong men, wanted to be seen at all the happening events, and spent more money on clothes than I could afford. I was trying to keep up with the Joneses and failing miserably. I ended up in serious debt and had to file for bankruptcy. I was thirty-one and my life was a mess.

Change was hard. Even as I stood on the promise I'd made to my dad, it was hard. Each day I woke up focused on changing my life. The best compliment I received during that time was, "You've changed," even if it was often not meant as a compliment. Regardless, it was a testament to my slow and steady transformation. I knew I was moving in the right direction because people saw the changes.

I also realized that I was lying to myself about why I was so determined to be successful. I had to change what was motivating me. Every time I accomplished another goal, I would think about the people that told me I would never amount to anything. That was unhealthy and not sustainable. I changed my mindset to only focus on the positive.

THEM

Recently, I worked with a group of companies that needed to attract and retain more diverse talent. I asked the people in the room to raise their hand if they believed they had the power to change their environment. Only one hand went up. Most times we know the problem, we have a great idea to change the problem, but we don't know who can help us change the situation. Without a change agent that has influence, nothing, including change, will happen.

THEM is harder to change!

What needs to change in your current environment? The people or the culture? How can you change either? How can you be a change agent? Who can help you change the environment? How long will you give yourself? Are you willing to leave if change doesn't happen?

Once you identify what to change, find a small group of champions who can help you build a plan and process to begin to change the environment.

It won't happen overnight! But it will be worth the effort even if you can only incite a small change.

12-3-1

I spent **12** years at **3** different companies with the same (**1**) exact job title!
(My pay increased slightly but title and responsibility matter for growth)

I thought because I was in a new environment, the outcome would certainly be different. However, I eventually realized that I had to change in order to get a different outcome.

Once I changed my mindset, attitude, and approach, I was able to seamlessly implement my **SUCCESS** formula (next page). I went from Director to Vice President.

After 18 months as a VP, I was promoted to a Senior Vice President and I also authored two books in the process.

It took 3 more years to receive an honorary doctorate in Humane Letters, become an Executive Vice President, and release my third book.

MICHELE'S SUCCESS FORMULA

1 cup of Commitment to yourself

1 cup of Commitment to write out your goals once you have clarity about your current environment and what you want to achieve

1 cup of Champions

2 cups of Courage to ask for what you've earned

1 cup of Communication in writing so you have an undeniable paper trail (follow-up until you get a response)

1 cup of willingness to Change if that's what the Culture demands

10 cups of Circling your goals in prayer

WHEN YOU ARE WILLING TO UNDERSTAND, ACCEPT, AND EXECUTE CHANGE, ANYTHING IS POSSIBLE.

-STRATECHIC

"Uncoachable kids become unemployable adults. Let your kids get used to someone being tough on them. It's life. Get over it."
-Patrick Murphy
Alabama Softball

GET A COACH AND BE COACHABLE

To train or instruct (a team or player).

IT'S ABOUT DEPENDABILITY, CONSISTENCY, BEING COACHABLE AND
UNDERSTANDING WHAT YOU NEED TO DO TO IMPROVE.
-BILL BELICHICK

I've coached hundreds of people on strategy and how to achieve better results for their lives and businesses. The most important aspect of being a coach is being coachable.

Throughout my career, I've garnered feedback along the way. I asked hard questions even when the truth of the answers made me uncomfortable, exposed, or even felt inaccurate.

I asked questions such as, How am I doing? Could I have done things differently? How would you have handled the situation? Will I get promoted and when? What are my weaknesses and blind spots?

You have to ask the right person at the right time and be willing to accept the answer as their truth. Even if they aren't aligned with what you believe, there's a perception that exists that must be addressed. Plus, once you have answers, you can change the outcome and operate in facts. Please make sure you get your coaching and feedback in writing. It becomes a roadmap for growth.

COMPETITION

"they wanna see you do good, but never better than them. Remember that."

About a year ago, while helping a young lady on her business plan, I asked, "Who is your competition?" To which she replied, "No one." Competition exists in everything and while I don't always give it energy, I still accept it exists. It helps me build a story so I can present an advantage. It also helps me build a story based on all of the facts.

The other side of competition is more complex and can sometimes be a little less obvious. There was a really smart young man looking to make a move within his company. The company loved him and saw him as a great employee and an asset. As a matter of fact, he was so good, it actually hampered him from being added to the promotion list because they believed no one could fill his role. His competition was the company not having others in the pipeline. He was invaluable in his current role and competition became his own value to that team.

It proves that competition exists everywhere and we must remain cognizant of any and every impediment to our success. When you identify your replacement, it's much easier to move up. You remove any barriers blocking your path.

"If you're a true warrior, competition doesn't scare you. It makes you better."
-Andrew Whitworth

Who is your **COMPETITION:** people or the system?

What do you need to do to beat them or it?

Who can be your champion through the process?

Who is your replacement if you want to move or elevate?

CAPACITY

The maximum amount that something
can contain.
The ability or power to do,
experience, or understand something.

WHAT PEOPLE HAVE THE CAPACITY TO CHOOSE,
THEY HAVE THE ABILITY TO CHANGE.
-MADELEINE ALBRIGHT

Capacity is always relevant but becomes paramount in moments of stress, frustration, and discontent. It is about doing your job well while maintaining the right attitude and mindset when you are in the midst of a storm. It's being able to stand and smile in situations meant to upset and stifle you. It is not retaliating or being rude when you feel you have every right to give people a piece of your mind.

Before you reach your destination of greatness, your capacity will be tested and tried many times.

Capacity is about exercising self-control. You are in control of your destiny and you cannot allow one situation to change the outcome.

If you want to get ahead or move forward but face obstacles, get real with yourself while not exposing every negative thought or emotion you have about the situation.

Having a poor attitude is the #1 reason I've seen people passed over for professional and personal opportunities. It happens more often than lack of skill, resources, or timing. It is insurmountable.

You can be angry, just don't show it. **EVER!**

You can't afford to have the system assign you with negative labels. Instead, channel that anger into productivity.

Building Capacity Checklist:

- [ ] HAVE A GREAT ATTITUDE EVERY DAY.
  EVEN IF IT MEANS TAKING AN ACTING CLASS.

- [ ] HAVE AN OUTLET FOR YOUR FRUSTRATION AND CONCERNS.

- [ ] FIND SOMEONE YOU CAN TRUST WITH YOUR FEELINGS (AN ADVOCATE).
  IT'S BETTER IF THE PERSON IS OUTSIDE OF YOUR COMPANY BUT
  WITHIN THE SAME INDUSTRY SO THEY CAN RELATE AND UNDERSTAND.

- [ ] FIND SOMETHING TO BE THANKFUL FOR DAILY
  AND EXPRESS GRATITUDE.

- [ ] DON'T COMPLAIN.

- [ ] DON'T TAKE IT PERSONALLY.

- [ ] DO NOT REACT IMMEDIATELY.

- [ ] TAKE TIME TO UNDERSTAND YOUR OPTIONS.

- [ ] PRAY FOR PATIENCE AND CONTROL.

CONSISTENT

Acting or done in the same way over time, especially so as to be fair or accurate.

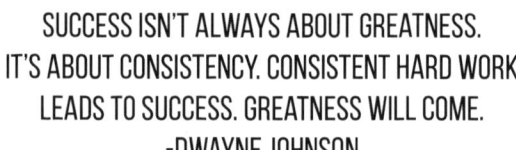

SUCCESS ISN'T ALWAYS ABOUT GREATNESS.
IT'S ABOUT CONSISTENCY. CONSISTENT HARD WORK
LEADS TO SUCCESS. GREATNESS WILL COME.
-DWAYNE JOHNSON

We hear it all time: **"Be consistent."** But what does that really mean and why is it so important? When I think about all of my accomplishments, none of them happened overnight. I'm not the most patient person so being consistent has helped me through those long patches of not getting the results I wanted right away.

Consistently be curious.

Stay consistent when you aren't getting the results you want right away.

Consistently check back in on your goals to make sure you are still aligned.

Consistently be kind.

Consistently evaluate your champions and friend circle.

Consistently be aware of your finances and live a life you can afford.

Consistently outwork everyone else.

Consistently be prepared.

Being consistent is a marathon, not a sprint.

Consistency is a daily routine.

Consistency relates to every aspect of life.

Consistency takes daily focus and discipline.

Commitment to Consistency is critical on the road to your success.

"If you are persistent, you will get it. If you are consistent, you will keep it."
–Harvey Mackay

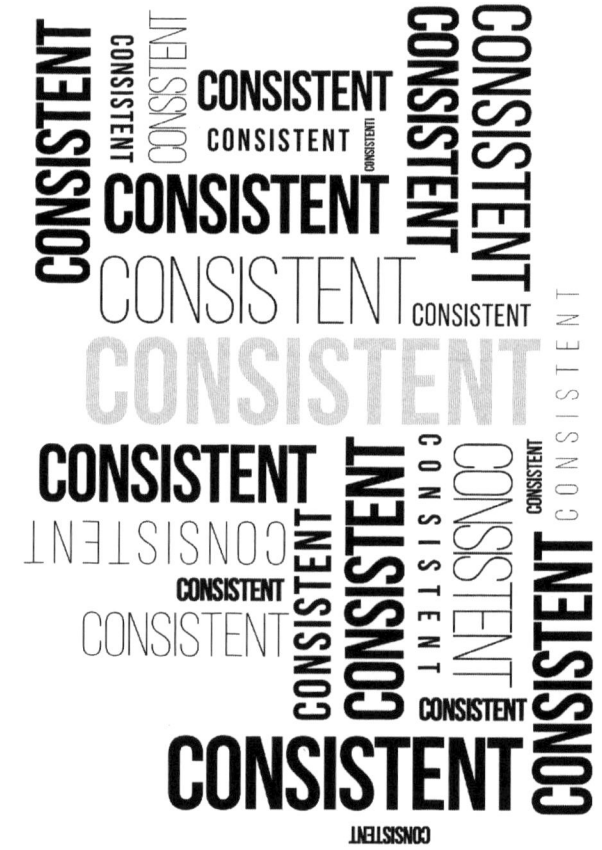

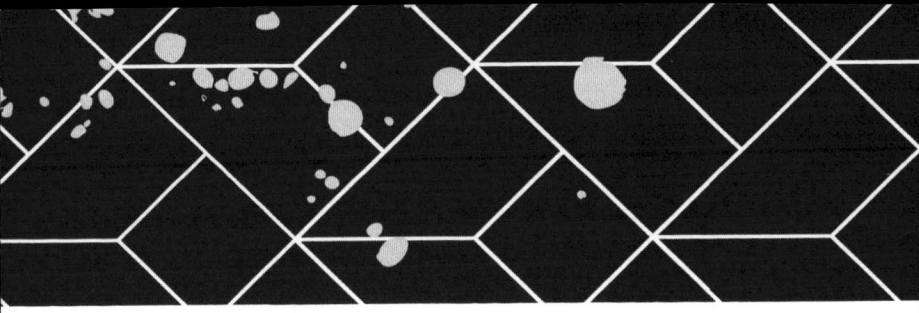

REFLECTION

What do I need to do consistently to be successful?

How often?

Make a list.

Create time in your day to accomplish each item.

Be consistent for the next 30 days.

Pray over your list.

CHAMPION

A person who fights or argues for a cause or on behalf of someone else.

SURROUND YOURSELF WITH PEOPLE WHO SUPPORT YOU. FIND CHAMPIONS.
-SARAH GAVRON

"I have always known that if you want to be successful at anything you do in life, you have to surround yourself with the people that are good at it. Training with champions makes you one."
– Nik Lentz

Yes, you need sponsors and advocates. But champions, however, know what it means to win and will fight on your behalf so you can win too.

I wanted to move to the next level in my company and if that wasn't going to happen, I would have to find the courage to leave and a champion to help make the move a reality.

I was recommended for my new role as an EVP by one of my greatest champions. Because the company knew she was a winner, there was a positive halo transferred onto me and with her as my champion, I was hired in record time.

Do you know your champions inside and outside of your personal and professional circles? How are you establishing and maintaining the relationship(s)?

5 Recommendations

1.   MAKE A LIST OF POSSIBLE CHAMPIONS.

2.   MAKE SURE THE LIST ONLY CONSISTS OF PEOPLE YOU KNOW WILL FIGHT ON YOUR BEHALF (CLARITY) AND THEY HAVE ENOUGH POWER TO MAKE SOMETHING HAPPEN.

3.   MAKE IT EASY FOR THEM BY SENDING EVERYTHING THEY NEED TO WORK ON YOUR BEHALF (RESUME, BIO, LETTERS, ETC.) AND SAVE THEM TIME BY DRAFTING EMAILS OR LETTERS IN ADVANCE SO THEY ONLY NEED TO MAKE TWEAKS.

4.   BE THE BEST AT WHAT YOU DO.

5.   BE THANKFUL AND LET THEM KNOW IT.

REMEMBER, THE FIRST THREE COMMUNICATION EFFORTS WITH YOUR CHAMPIONS SHOULD BE ABOUT <u>THEM AND THEIR NEEDS AND NOT ABOUT YOU AND YOUR WANTS.</u>

CONNECTIONS

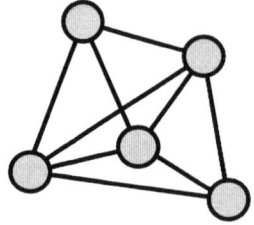

A relationship in which a person, thing, or idea is linked or associated with something else.

Think about who you are connected to and why. What value do you offer to their life and vice versa? How can you build your connections to be more meaningful and relevant in the short and long-term?

Do you have an idea of the role assigned to each person you are connected to or associated with? For your success, who is involved and who should be? On the other hand, whose success is directly and uniquely tied to you—your decisions, actions, and plans? Often, we casually move from one conversation to the next not understanding how to use the time to find or strengthen our connection with a current or potential advocate or to determine if we can advocate on someone else's behalf.

One trap is the **TRANSACTIONAL CONNECTION**. It is when you only communicate with someone when you need something. It comes across as disingenuous, selfish, and superficial. They are also short-term and may cause more damage than good. Try to understand what other people need and be a resource instead of a drain. Find ways to help them without only thinking about how they can help or benefit you.

Another positive outcome to having meaningful associations is the ability to be a connector. Become someone that solves problems for others by introducing people and creating relationships that address their biggest challenges.

Connections and associations matter. Do you have the right connections to help you realize the success you've been dreaming of?

✔ **Connect** with people that you respect.

✔ **Connect** with people in and out of your field.

✔ **Connect** with like-minded people.

✔ Use social media and digital tools to make **Connections**. (And follow up 10 times)

✔ **Connect** with those that add value to your life and vice versa.

✔ **Connect** beyond the transactional.

✔ Be a **Connector** for others so they can also succeed.

✔ Stay in regular communication with your **Connections**.

✔ Volunteer to meet new **Connections** authentically.

✔ Send your **Connections** valuable information they can use.

"The harder the conflict, the more glorious the triumph."
-Thomas Paine

CONFLICT

A serious disagreement or argument.

WHENEVER YOU'RE IN CONFLICT WITH SOMEONE, THERE IS ONE FACTOR THAT CAN MAKE THE DIFFERENCE BETWEEN DAMAGING YOUR RELATIONSHIP AND DEEPENING IT. THAT FACTOR IS ATTITUDE.
-WILLIAM JAMES

True leadership is tested in conflict.

Once you communicate in writing and people respond, you create an agreement and roadmap for follow-up. Whenever I hear that someone isn't getting what they've earned, my first question is, "Have you documented your contributions, successes, and wants?" If you haven't, you won't get it. Period!

Take the time right now to draft a letter to yourself with what you have accomplished, how you are valuable/ unique, and what you want.

CONFLICT IS NECESSARY.

How we react in moments of conflict is important to our success. Attitude is the key factor to how we win. Conflict and capacity are closely related.

How To Resolve Conflict

When **CONFLICT** arises:

Never respond immediately.

Identify the core issue.

Be empathetic and put yourself in the other person's shoes.

Communicate. Communicate. Communicate.

Never put anything in writing that you may one day regret.

Don't take it personally--unless it is personal.

Exercise capacity.

Accept Conflict as the price of SUCCESS.

YOU DO NOT HAVE TO LIKE PEOPLE, YOU JUST HAVE TO RESPECT THEM.

COMMUNICATE

Share or exchange information, news, or ideas.

THE BIGGEST COMMUNICATION PROBLEM IS WE DO NOT LISTEN TO
UNDERSTAND.
WE LISTEN TO REPLY.
-STEPHEN COVEY

COMMUNICATION
STARTS WITH LISTENING.

First, start by finding out how people perceive you. Don't ask people like your subordinates (or even your boss) who may have their own reasons for not telling you the truth. Instead, ask people who don't have a stake in whether you win or lose. Get opinions from people you come across daily in both professional and personal situations. Talk to **ADMINISTRATIVE ASSISTANTS**, mail room clerks, friends, family members, advisors, receptionist, etc. Get a well-rounded view of how people perceive you so you can understand if there's a gap between that and how you want to be perceived.

"TAKE ADVANTAGE OF EVERY OPPORTUNITY TO PRACTICE YOUR COMMUNICATION SKILLS SO THAT WHEN IMPORTANT OCCASIONS ARISE, YOU WILL HAVE THE GIFT, THE STYLE, THE SHARPNESS, THE CLARITY, AND THE EMOTIONS TO AFFECT OTHER PEOPLE."
- JIM ROHN

Several years ago, I hired a voice and diction coach to better enable me to communicate my wants, desires, and thoughts. The better I became, the more people understood and the more I got what I wanted. I wrote my personal mission statement and spent hours practicing it in the mirror. When I do something great or I'm acknowledged with an award, I communicate that message to the right people at the right time.

Back in 2017, I had just won a big award and I asked the communications department to announce it to the entire company. I had worked hard and the industry honored me. Shouldn't the company I worked for also recognize and celebrate my achievement? Shouldn't I benefit, as well as my company, for my accomplishment as one of their executives? If no one knows what you're doing, how can that benefit your growth?

One week went by and no announcement. Then another week went by and still no announcement. So, I decided to take matters into my own hands. I crafted the following email to executives within the company:

Subject: Thank you for allowing women in the company to excel.

Body of the email: I want to thank you for allowing me to work in an environment that encourages women to take risks and be creative. Today, the marketplace recognized me as an industry titan. You should be proud of our leadership. Thank you.

From the beginning, starting with the subject line, it was strategic. They were more likely to read an email with that subject because I'd made it about them. The CEO of our company responded immediately and his direct reports followed suit. I had a response in writing from the highest level of our company that I deserved the recognition because of my contribution. The communications team immediately sent out a company-wide congratulations email. Had I not sent an email and worded my message to the executive team in a way that required a response, I would have never received one.

COMMUNICATION checklist

- ✔ Write your 60-second narrative.
- ✔ Practice your narrative daily (in the shower, in your car, at your desk).
- ✔ Record yourself and listen.
- ✔ Practice in front of friends and ask for feedback.
- ✔ Hire a coach to help you perfect your communication skills.
- ✔ Learn to communicate with people you don't like.
- ✔ Communicate information to the right people at the right time.
- ✔ Learn how to effectively communicate in writing.
- ✔ Know when to communicate in writing.
- ✔ Never communicate when you are angry. **NEVER.**
- ✔ Don't be afraid to ask for things you've earned and communicate it to a meaningful audience.

WHEN YOU KNOW YOUR STORY
AND CAN **COMMUNICATE** IT
TO THE RIGHT PEOPLE
AT THE RIGHT TIME,
ANYTHING IS **POSSIBLE!**

CURIOSITY

A strong desire to know or learn something.

WE KEEP MOVING FORWARD, OPENING NEW DOORS, AND DOING NEW THINGS, BECAUSE WE'RE CURIOUS AND CURIOSITY KEEPS LEADING US DOWN NEW PATHS.
-WALT DISNEY

You can't be successful without wanting to grow and learn about new and different things.

Curiosity is more important today than it has ever been. With an ever-present **24/7** news cycle and fast-paced changes in technology impacting the world more and more with each passing day, we must stay abreast of current trends. Curiosity is the gas that fuels that desire. It allows us to stay relevant by asking questions and wanting more.

Most importantly, it leaves the impression on others that we are in the game to play and to **WIN**.

When you stop asking and
learning, you stop growing and
W I N N I N G ! !

CURIOSITY checklist

- ✅ Know your company.

- ✅ Visit the website weekly.

- ✅ Set up Google alerts on your company, important clients, and yourself.

- ✅ Ask at least 1 question each week (in a meeting or via email) based on the information.

- ✅ Stay on top of trends in the marketplace.

- ✅ Know your co-workers.

- ✅ Be curious about your industry and beyond.

CREATIVITY

Relating to or involving the imagination or original ideas.

CREATIVITY IS JUST CONNECTING THINGS. WHEN YOU ASK CREATIVE PEOPLE HOW THEY DID SOMETHING, THEY FEEL A LITTLE GUILTY BECAUSE THEY DIDN'T REALLY DO IT, THEY JUST SAW SOMETHING. SOMETHING THAT SEEMED OBVIOUS TO THEM AFTER A WHILE. THAT'S BECAUSE THEY WERE ABLE TO CONNECT EXPERIENCES THEY'VE HAD AND SYNTHESIZE NEW THINGS.
-STEVE JOBS

CREATIVITY allowed me to remove myself from the status quo.

You don't have to be creative to **CREATE** great content.

You need time and energy to **CREATE.**

CREATIVITY moves you ahead of your competition.

CREATIVITY allowed me to shine.

CREATIVITY got me promoted three times.

I paid attention to my environment and asked what was possible. What did the marketplace need that we could provide? I asked what I wanted to see based on my own life experiences. That's how I came up with **BETHer**, the first network for black women. I wanted a network for me and my friends and I knew advertisers needed a direct vehicle to sell black women products and services. I also knew that black women watched more content across all screens than any other demographic. A quantifiable revenue model was tied to my idea. In the end, the network was welcomed by the marketplace, advertisers, and viewers.

Get in your own way with your own crazy creative ideas and test them to see if they are valuable. When they tell you no, be creative and rephrase the question to get a yes. They must not have understood the question.

COMPASSION

Sympathy and concern for the suffering or misfortunes of others.

LOVE AND COMPASSION ARE NECESSITIES, NOT LUXURIES. WITHOUT THEM, HUMANITY CANNOT SURVIVE.
-DALAI LAMA

Compassion is a key factor to **SUCCESS**. The more compassionate you are, the more you are willing to work with others and want to help them be better. Compassion begins with gratitude. The more grateful you are, the more compassion you show. The side effect to compassion is a more successful environment.

Michele's Recommendations

- Ask God to give you a heart of Compassion.

- Do something every day to help someone else.

- Be empathetic. Imagine what it might be like to walk a mile in another person's shoes.

- Give to those in need.

- Try listening more and talking less.

- Acknowledge people in your school, company, or community that rarely, if ever, get recognized.

- Give and expect nothing in return.

Two jobs taught me a lot about hard work, compassion, and gratitude--working at the front desk of a hotel and cleaning houses. At the time, I noticed how much people talked down to me and my coworkers and treated us like we had no feelings and no future. Going through those experiences shifted something in me that I will never, ever forget. It's why I walk with compassion everyday and don't judge someone else's journey. Whether I'm in a meeting, with my friends, or out in public, I treat others with kindness and respect.

When I stay at a hotel, I always leave a gratuity for the cleaning professionals because I want them to know, "I See You."

COMMUNITY SERVICE

Volunteer work intended to help people in a particular area.

SERVICE TO OTHERS IS THE RENT YOU PAY FOR YOUR ROOM HERE ON EARTH.
— MUHAMMAD ALI

I volunteer because I was raised to give back. I didn't realize what it would give to me in return—leadership skills, ability to read financial statements, business development, fundraising, and connections.

Corporate America said I wasn't experienced. I was told "no" for jobs because I lacked certain skills. Although I said, "I can learn on the job," they were not having it. Offering my time and volunteering to sit on boards allowed me to fill in all the blanks on my resume and took away their "no." I recommend you volunteer where there will be an alignment between your passion and career. Find areas that you are both passionate about and help you with attaining necessary skills to progress in the rest of your life. I remember asking where the executives in my company volunteered. I found one that aligned with my passion. I was able to build a great relationship with that executive because we bonded outside of work.

"I'VE LEARNED THAT YOU SHOULDN'T GO THROUGH LIFE WITH A CATCHER'S MITT ON BOTH HANDS. YOU NEED TO BE ABLE TO THROW SOMETHING BACK."
— MAYA ANGELOU

WE MAKE A LIVING BY WHAT WE GET;
WE MAKE A LIFE BY WHAT WE GIVE.
— WINSTON CHURCHILL

"Life's most persistent and urgent question is,
What are you doing for others?"
-Martin Luther King Jr.

Things to Consider

What skills are you lacking?

Where are you currently volunteering?

What do you have to offer and what can you learn?

When and how will you make contact with the organization?

In what organizations do the executives at your company serve? Is that something you are passionate about? If so, how do you sign up?

How much time during the week can you allocate to the community?

What organizations fit your passion and ALSO align with your industry?

What skills can you develop by volunteering?

How will you identify which organization makes sense for you?

What's your process for following through?

CHOICE

An act of selecting or making a decision when faced with two or more possibilities.

Every day is a choice.

I've had to make some really tough decisions in my lifetime. I didn't go to school right after college and that single **CHOICE** set me on a path of one poor decision after another. At 31, my dad passed away and I made him a promise that I would make something of my life. I began to understand the power to choose. To not sit on the sidelines and let life pass you by.

I choose to be a working mom. I also choose to have a no-guilt policy. My children understand that we all have choices and it's our responsibility to choose or the outcome will be chosen for us.

Approximately 80% of the decisions that impact our lives happen in rooms in which we aren't invited and during conversations that do not include us. Therefore, we must choose for ourselves and not allow life, the past, people, circumstances, or anything else to make the choice for us. ***Choice gives you control!***

We choose if we want to live a successful life. We choose what success looks like for us. We choose the time we give to unworthy people and we choose to remove those same people from our lives. We choose the attitude we exude and we choose the reaction we have when things don't go our way. We must choose to do something every day to reach our goals and dreams.

We must choose:

To always be prepared

To stay positive when things go wrong

To believe people when they show us who they are

To walk in faith and not fear

To be happy

To be kind

To fight when things look bleak

To listen more than talk

To stay humble

To be thankful in good times and bad

To say *No* to them and *Yes* to yourself

To leave when there's no opportunity for growth

TO ASK FOR WHAT WE'VE EARNED!

<u>WE</u>, <u>US</u>, <u>ME</u>, <u>YOU</u>—have the choice to be successful.

So what choices are you going to make today to get yours!

CELEBRATE

Acknowledge (a significant or happy day or event) with a social gathering or enjoyable activity.

I WILL NOT WAIT FOR OTHERS TO ACKNOWLEDGE MY GREATNESS. I WILL CELEBRATE MYSELF WHEN THE TIME IS APPROPRIATE. CONSISTENTLY AND WITH COURAGE.

There are so many times that I accomplished something and did not stop to enjoy the achievement. Or that I garnered some type of recognition and didn't take the time to celebrate me. Not in a bragging or boastful way but in a way that makes me understand that I have accomplished something.

We have to take time to really **CELEBRATE** ourselves!

We have to take time to celebrate others that deserve it.

When you reach each level of SUCCESS: ON YOUR TERMS, CELEBRATE!

I saved the best for last.
Because, without Christ, I am nothing.

I have been through trials and tribulations
not shared with anyone other than God.
He has been my rock—my fortress—and
I am absolutely positive there is no
SUCCESS, without Him!

CIRCLE

No weapon penetrates this circle. The enemy has no dominion over my life, my family, or my **SUCCESS**.

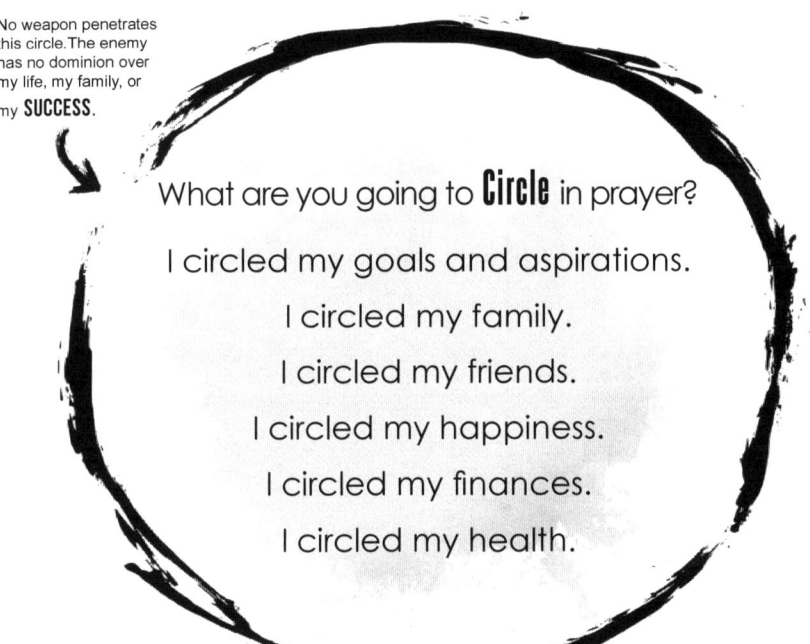

What are you going to **Circle** in prayer?

I circled my goals and aspirations.

I circled my family.

I circled my friends.

I circled my happiness.

I circled my finances.

I circled my health.

God, I pray that you circle every person reading this book. I pray you bring clarity to their wants and needs. Help them define success for themselves. True success that brings joy, happiness, and fulfillment. The type of success that doesn't need validation from anyone else. I pray for their big, audacious prayers. In Jesus' name. **Amen.**

The **CIRCLE** checklist

- ✅ Read *The Circle Maker* by Mark Batterson.

- ✅ Make a list of all the success you want in your life and post it on your wall/wherever you will see it. Kneel before it and pray circles around it.

- ✅ Draw prayer circles around it every day.

- ✅ Believe you deserve it.

- ✅ Stand on God's promise.

- ✅ Be prepared to walk in it.

- ✅ Ask God to close the doors not meant for you.

"CHARACTER CANNOT BE DEVELOPED IN EASE AND QUIET. ONLY THROUGH EXPERIENCE OF TRIAL AND SUFFERING CAN THE SOUL BE STRENGTHENED, AMBITION INSPIRED, AND SUCCESS ACHIEVED."
-HELEN KELLER

Be your version of success through God!

We love our comfort; God prefers our faith.
We love predictability; God invites us on an
adventure. We want relief; God wants redemption.
We want a break; God is after a breakthrough.

Hidden in every trying circumstance is an opportunity
to experience God, to engage our faith, and to see
Him move. More often than not, we ask too little from
God. He's greater, grander, and more magnificent
than we can imagine. And He'll waste nothing. He's
using every nuance of your story to make you into
someone you never dreamed you could be.

Pray Big. Dream Big. Take Risks. God will lead you
on the best path for your life.

-Susie Larson

A Final Word from Michele

Thank you for choosing to define **SUCCESS On Your Terms**! Although this is the end of the book, it is the beginning of your journey.
It's time for you to choose what happens next.
What does **SUCCESS** mean for your life?

My definition of success starts within my household. I won't be a success unless my family is protected and my children are the best version of themselves. For me, success means having this book, along with the other two that I've written, change lives. My view of **SUCCESS** is bigger than a job or a title. I want my success to impact the world!

— Michele

www.michelethorntonghee.com

@Stratechic